I'm Allergic to School!

Robert Pottle

Illustrated by
Mike & Carl Gordon

Ⓜ Meadowbrook Press
Distributed by Simon & Schuster
New York

Contents

I Stapled My Shirt to My Shoelace

(sing to the tune of "My Bonnie")

I stapled my shirt to my shoelace,
invented a crazy new dance.
I cut off my sleeves with the scissors,
then shredded the legs of my pants.

Chorus
I think school's fun.
I really like going to school—it's cool!
I think school's fun.
I really like going to school!

I covered my zipper with glitter,
and then I decided to taste
a crayon, the chalk, and some paper,
a pen, an eraser, and paste.

Chorus

I painted a face on my belly.
I drew a blue beard on my chin.
My first day of school was so much fun,
I can't wait to do it again!

Chorus

The Kindergarten Concert

The kindergarten concert was an interesting show.
Peter walked onto the stage and yelled, "I have to go!"
Katie was embarrassed, but she had nowhere to hide.
She raised her dress to hide her face. Her mother almost died.
Keith removed his tie and said, "It's ugly, Dad. I hate it!"
David picked his nose on stage. What's worse is that he ate it.
They sang their song, and Wyatt burped, and then he did a dance.
Michael fell while spinning 'round. Peter wet his pants.
The music teacher at the end said, "There, I'm glad that's done."
The kindergarten bowed and said, "Let's sing another one!"

I'm a Toilet-Paper Mummy

(sing to the tune of "I'm a Yankee Doodle Dandy")

I'm a toilet-paper mummy.
I'm running up and down the hall.
And when my classmates take a look at me,
they laugh so hard that they fall.
With twenty-seven rolls of paper
I am brilliantly disguised.
    Toilet paper everywhere
    from foot to face to fanny.
Oh, won't my teacher be surprised!

When I run into the classroom,
I hear the kids begin to shout.
They say,"Let's all dress like mummies, too!"
They leave to go try it out.
And when they come back from the bathroom,
I am laughing in a fit.
     All of us are mummies now.
     We're running 'round the classroom.
I think my teacher wants to quit!

Allergic

I'm allergic to pencils,
allergic to ink,
allergic to markers
and crayons, I think.

I'm allergic to homework,
allergic to rules.
To sum it all up:
I'm allergic to schools.

I Overslept This Morning

I overslept this morning. I jumped up out of bed.
I put on different-colored socks: one blue, the other red.
I put my shirt on backward and forgot to zip my fly.
I scratched my mom behind her ears, then kissed the dog goodbye.
I ran to get to school on time. My foot soon had a bruise.
I guess that's just what happens when you don't wear any shoes.
I got to school. The door was locked, much to my dismay.
I can't believe that I forgot today is Saturday.

I Wrote a Book

I wrote a book at school today.
I wrote it in a minute.
You only need a second
to read everything that's in it.
It doesn't have a single word.
It has no illustrations.

My teacher tried to grade it,
which caused numerous frustrations.
The kids sure like the book I wrote.
They say it's really cool.
The title of my blank-paged book
is "What I've Learned at School."

Gotta Go!

I gotta go! I gotta go!
I'll ask the teacher first.
I gotta go! I gotta go!
I think I'm gonna burst.

I gotta go! I gotta go!
I'd better raise my hand.
I gotta go! I gotta go!
But maybe I should stand.

I gotta go! I gotta go!
My hand is raised up high.
I gotta go! I gotta go!
I hope my pants stay dry.

I gotta go! I gotta go!
I'm really in a bind.
I gotta go! I gotta—
Uh-oh. Never mind.

11

What I've Learned at School

At school I've learned a lot of things
I really like to do,
like running in the hallway
and eating gobs of glue.
I've learned I'm good at making pencils
dangle from my nose.
I've learned to hum and pop my gum.
I practice, and it shows.
I've learned I like to cut in line
and love to cut the cheese.
I've learned to fake a burp, a cough,
and even fake a sneeze.
You'd think with all this learning
I'd be doing well in school,
but everything I learn to do
appears to break a rule.

I Ain't Been to School

I ain't been to school,
not never before.
That's all changin' now
as I run through the door.

I drool on my worksheet
then chew on a book.
I eat off the floor
and growl at the cook.

I drink from the toilet.
I spill all the glue.
I lick my new teacher
and leak on her shoe.

The principal says that
I broke every rule.
I just learnt the reason
dogs can't go to school.

Kenny Had a Camera

Kenny had a camera and took pictures while we ate.
I thought it might be fun to use my food to decorate.
I grabbed a brown banana peel and used it for a wig,
dangled French fries from my nose and snorted like a pig.
I took some veggies from my tray and stuck them in my ears.
I knew that I looked funny 'cause the room soon filled with cheers.
But best at being funny was my teacher, I suppose,
'cause when she looked and laughed at me, milk came out her nose.

There's a Puddle on the Playground

(sing to the tune of "The Battle Hymn of the Republic")

We went outside for recess. It was time to run and play.
Oh, but everything was wet because it rained the other day.
So we found a giant puddle, and I heard my buddy say,
"It's time to have some fun!"

Chorus
There's a puddle on the playground.
There's a puddle on the playground.
There's a puddle on the playground.
It's time to have some fun!

The teacher looked the other way. I knew it was my chance.
So I jumped into the puddle, and I did a crazy dance.
Oh, I got some water in my boots and then I soaked my pants.
It's time to have some fun!

Chorus

My teacher looked and saw me, then she started coming near.
Well, I knew I was in trouble, and my heart was filled with fear
till she jumped into the puddle, and she said, "I'm glad I'm here.
It's time to have some fun!"

Chorus

I Ripped My Pants at School Today

I ripped my pants at school today
while going down the slide.
It wasn't just a little tear.
I ripped 'em open wide.

Now everyone at school can see
my purple underwear.
Although the sight makes people laugh,
I'm glad I've got them there.

Every Swing Is Being Used

Every swing is being used,
and no one wants to share.
The soccer game is way too rough.
I'd play, but I don't dare.

The twirl-a-whirl is spinning 'round
so fast it's just a blur.
I walked up to the seesaw
and was greeted with a "*Grrrrr.*"

I'm told that I cannot play tag.
The climbing wall is crowded.
I said that we should all take turns,
but everybody pouted.

The giant slide has got a line.
Oh, what a rotten day!
It's no fun on the playground
when the teachers get to play.

Peewee Soccer

Christopher is counting clouds.
Hannah braids her hair.
Peter's playing peekaboo.
Greg growls like a bear.

Kevin kicks with all his might,
and though the ball stays put,
his sneaker sails across the field
to land near Roger's foot.

Roger starts to kick the shoe.
And soon poor Kevin's crying.
Katie gives the ball a kick
and sends that ball a-flying.

Billy Brown is looking down.
He sees a four-leaf clover.
Billy wants to pick the plant,
and that's why he bends over.

We see the ball bounce off his bum
and then sail toward the goal.
The goalie gets confused.
We watch him stop then drop and roll.

The other team lets out a cheer
and our team starts to scream
as Billy's bottom scores a goal
for the other team.

I Brought My Grandma's Teeth to School

I brought my grandma's teeth to school to share for show-and-tell.
Billy showed his sneakers. It was more like show-and-*smell*.

Kevin brought a violin and showed he couldn't play.
Katie brought her snake to school—too bad it got away.
Our class likes show-and-tell a lot, so we were sad to hear
our teacher say that show-and-tell is canceled till next year.

Our Poor Teacher

(sing to the tune of "London Bridge")

Our poor teacher wears a frown,
wears a frown, wears a frown.
Our poor teacher wears a frown.
She's not happy.

All the kids are acting up,
acting up, acting up.
All the kids are acting up,
misbehaving.

Larry ate the teacher's lunch,
teacher's lunch, teacher's lunch.
Larry ate the teacher's lunch
and her apple.

Jennifer jumps up and down,
up and down, up and down.
Jennifer jumps up and down
in the trash can.

Roger reads the answer key,
answer key, answer key.
Roger reads the answer key
for our math test.

Julie-Anna scrapes her nails,
scrapes her nails, scrapes her nails.
Julie-Anna scrapes her nails
on the chalkboard.

Our poor teacher's going home,
going home, going home.
Our poor teacher's going home
with a headache.

We will have a substitute,
substitute, substitute.
We will have a substitute—
our next victim!

The Bus

Sixty kids and one adult—
you gotta love those odds.
The perfect place for pulling pranks
and throwing paper wads.
Hank is standing on his head.
Billy's playing ball.
Peter wet his pants again.
Tasha pushes Paul.

Steven steals. Kevin cries.
Millicent is missing.
Katie punched her cousin Keith.
Ben and Jen are kissing.
Me, I'm taking lots of notes
on public transportation.
I think the bus provides me with
the finest education.

The More I Do My Homework

(sing to the tune of "The More We Get Together" or "Did You Ever See a Lassie?")

Oh, when I'm in my classroom,
my classroom, my classroom,
yes, when I'm in my classroom
I fall sound asleep.
I'm snoring and drooling
from all of this schooling.
'Cause when I'm in my classroom
I fall sound asleep.

The more I do my homework,
my homework, my homework,
the more I do my homework
the sleepier I get.
'Cause homework is boring.
It makes me start snoring.
The more I do my homework
the sleepier I get.

But now that it's my bedtime,
my bedtime, my bedtime,
yes, now that it's my bedtime,
I feel wide awake.
At school I was tired,
but now I feel wired.
Oh, now that it's my bedtime
I feel wide awake.

Library of Congress Cataloging-in-Publication Data

Pottle, Robert.
  I'm allergic to school! : funny poems and songs about school / by Robert Pottle; Illustrated by Mike and Carl Gordon.
      p. cm.
  Summary:"A collection of hilarious songs and poems about the funny things that happen at school" —Provided by publisher.
  ISBN 0-88166-522-3 (Meadowbrook Press) ISBN 1-4169-2947-9 (Simon & Schuster)
  1. Schools—Juvenile poetry. 2. Children's poetry, American. I. Gordon, Mike. II. Gordon, Carl. III. Title.
  PS3616.O856I6 2007
  811'.6—dc22
                        2006007012

Project Director: Bruce Lansky
Editorial Director: Christine Zuchora-Walske
Coordinating Editor and Copyeditor: Angela Wiechmann
Proofreader and Editorial Assistant: Alicia Ester
Production Manager: Paul Woods
Graphic Design Manager: Tamara Peterson
Illustrations and Cover Art: Mike and Carl Gordon

© 2007 by Robert Pottle

Published by Meadowbrook Press, 5451 Smetana Drive, Minnetonka, Minnesota 55343

www.meadowbrookpress.com

BOOK TRADE DISTRIBUTION by Simon and Schuster, a division of Simon and Schuster, Inc.,
1230 Avenue of the Americas, New York, New York 10020

12 11 10 09 08 07   10 9 8 7 6 5 4 3 2 1

Printed in China

Acknowledgments

Many thanks to the following teachers and their students who tested poems for this collection:
Marianne Gately, McCarthy Elementary, Framingham, MA
Pamela Greer, East Elementary, New Richmond, WI
Sandy Kane, Lincoln Elementary, Faribault, MN
Carmen Markgren, East Elementary, New Richmond, WI
John Pundsack, East Elementary, New Richmond, WI
Ruth Refsnider, East Elementary, New Richmond, WI
Beverly Semanko, Rum River Elementary, Andover, MN
Maria Smith, Deer Creek Elementary, Crowley, TX
Margaret Weiss, East Elementary, New Richmond, WI